222517

D0805564

BL

Pts. 5

Sound

by **Becky Olien**

Consultant:
Philip W. Hammer, Ph.D.
Vice President, The Franklin Center
The Franklin Institute Science Museum

Bridgestone Books
an imprint of Capstone Press
Mankato, Minnesota

Bridgestone Books are published by Capstone Press
151 Good Counsel Drive, P.O. Box 669, Mankato, Minnesota 56002
http://www.capstone-press.com

Library of Congress Cataloging-in-Publication Data
Olien, Rebecca.
    Sound/by Becky Olien.
    p. cm.—(Our physical world)
    Includes bibliographical references and index.
    Summary: Introduces sound and hearing, and provides instructions for an activity to
demonstrate some of their characteristics.
    ISBN 0-7368-1407-8 (hardcover)
    1. Sound—Juvenile literature. [1. Sound.] I. Title. II. Series.
QC225.5 .O45 2003
534—dc21   2001007890

Editorial Credits
Erika Mikkelson, editor; Karen Risch, product planning editor; Linda Clavel, designer;
    Anne McMullen, illustrator; Alta Schaffer, photo researcher

Photo Credits
Capstone Press/Jim Foell, 21
Hulton/Archive by Getty Images, 19
Jay Ireland and Georgienne E. Ireland, 7
PhotoDisc, Inc., cover
Skjold Photographs, 11, 15
Stephanie Maze/CORBIS, 5
Unicorn Stock Photos/Nancy P. Alexander, 17
Visuals Unlimited, 8; Fritz Pölking, 9; George Herben, 10; Jeannette Thomas, 13;
    Jeff Greenberg, 14

1 2 3 4 5 6 07 06 05 04 03 02

Table of Contents

Sound

Sound is a form of energy. Energy gives things the ability to move or do work. Objects make sounds when they move. Beating a drum vibrates the air. The moving air is called a sound wave. You hear sound when the wave enters your ear.

5

Sound Travels

Sound travels in waves. Sound waves travel through air, water, and solids. A person's voice travels through air. Whales send sounds to each other in the ocean. Sounds travel faster in water than in air. Sounds travel best in solids. Metal pipes can carry sound waves long distances.

solid
a hard, firm object
that takes up space

High and Low Sounds

Sounds can have a high or low pitch. Fast vibrations make high-pitched sounds. A bird chirps a high sound. Air in its throat vibrates fast.

FUN FACT

People cannot hear all sounds. Dogs hear sounds too high for people to hear. Elephants communicate with sounds too low for human ears.

Slow vibrations make low-pitched sounds.
A lion's roar is low. The air in a lion's throat
vibrates slowly.

pitch
the highness or
lowness of a sound

9

Loud and Quiet Sounds

Sounds have different volumes. A loud sound has a high volume. Big sound waves make louder sounds. Loud sounds vibrate more air than quiet sounds.

Sounds are louder when they are close.
Sounds become quieter as sound waves
travel farther away.

Sound Bounces

Sound waves bounce off surfaces. An echo is a sound wave bouncing back to where it was made. Someone yelling in a canyon hears an echo. Scientists use echoes to measure how deep the ocean is. Echoes take longer to return where the ocean is deep.

FUN FACT

Oceanographers study oceans. These scientists use computers and other equipment to send sound waves into the ocean. Oceanographers then listen to the echo from the sound waves bouncing off the ocean floor.

13

Making Sounds

People make sounds. Vocal cords in the throat vibrate. Vocal cords stretch and shrink to make sounds.

14

TRY THIS!

Place two fingers against your throat. Speak quietly. Now try singing loudly. Did you feel your vocal cords vibrate?

People play instruments to make music.
Instruments use vibration to make sounds. Air
blown inside a trombone vibrates to make music.

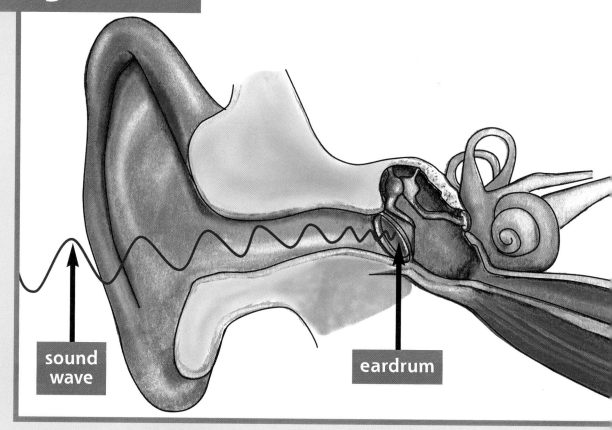

sound wave

eardrum

Sound waves enter the ears of people and animals. A thin skin called an eardrum is inside each ear. Sound waves vibrate the eardrum.

16

The eardrum sends vibrations farther
into the ear. These vibrations carry sound
messages to the brain.

Alexander Graham Bell

In 1876, Alexander Graham Bell invented the telephone. Thomas Watson helped him. They found a way to change the human voice into electric signals. The signals then traveled through wires. At the end of the wire, the signals turned back into sound waves.

Sound Safety

Loud sounds are dangerous. They hurt people's ears and can cause hearing loss. Turn the volume down low when watching TV. Use low volume when listening to the radio. Never shout in someone's ear.

Hands On: How Bells Ring

Bells are used to call people together, warn of danger, and make music. This activity shows you how they work.

What You Need

String
Scissors
Empty coffee can
Tape
Penny

What You Do

1. Cut a piece of string shorter than the height of the coffee can.
2. Tape one end of the string to the penny.
3. Tape the other end inside the bottom of the coffee can.
4. Turn the coffee can upside down. The penny should hang inside the coffee can.
5. Hold the can near the bottom. Tip the can back and forth to make the bell ring. Try holding the can different ways to make the loudest sound.
6. Wrap both hands around the sides of the can and try to ring the bell. The bell will only make a clunking sound.

Bells ring because their outsides vibrate when hit with the clapper. Your bell uses a penny as a clapper. The can vibrates to make a ringing sound when the clapper hits the sides. Wrapping your hands around the can stops the vibrations.

Words to Know

communicate (kuh-MYOO-nuh-kate)—to send and receive messages

eardrum (EEHR-druhm)—a thin skin inside the ear; the eardrum vibrates when sound waves enter the ear.

energy (EN-ur-jee)—the ability to move things or do work

instrument (IN-struh-muhnt)—something used to make music

pitch (PICH)—the highness or lowness of a sound

vibrate (VYE-brate)—to move back and forth quickly; sound is made when air vibrates.

vocal cords (VOH-kuhl KORDS)—part of the throat used to make sound

volume (VOL-yuhm)—the loudness of a sound

Read More

Cobb, Vicki. *Bangs and Twangs: Science Fun with Sound.* Brookfield, Conn.: Millbrook Press, 2000.

Pfeffer, Wendy. *Sounds All Around.* Let's-Read-and-Find-Out Science. New York: HarperCollins, 1999.

Wright, Lynne. *The Science of Noise.* Science World. Austin, Texas: Raintree Steck-Vaughn, 2000.

Internet Sites

BrainPOP: Sound
http://www.brainpop.com/science/sound
Sound Safaris
http://www.wildsanctuary.com/safari.html
The Sound Site
http://www.smm.org/sound

Index